EDINBURGH COME ALL YE

POEMS

BY

ALAN SPENCE

Scotland Street Press

EDINBURGH

First Published in the UK in 2022 by

Scotland Street Press

100 Willowbrae Avenue

Edinburgh EH8 7HU

Second edtion 2023

A CIP record for this book is available from the British Library.

ISBN 978-1-910895-66-5

Typeset and cover design by Antonia Shack in Edinburgh

Cover image *Wells of Arthur's Seat, St Anthony's Chapel from St Margaret's Loch* by Rose Strang

Contents

List of Artworks

Introduction

Most of the poems in this collection were written during my term as Edinburgh Makar, the Poet Laureate for the City, from 2017 to 2021.

The original appointment was for three years, extended by a year as the Covid pandemic curtailed activity, with public events and commissioned work seriously cut back. Until then I had done a fair bit of both, and I have to say I really enjoyed the ambassadorial aspect of the role - getting up in front of 400 folk at the Town Hall in Krakow, for instance, reading a poem I'd been asked to write to celebrate the city's links with Edinburgh. Or taking part in *Den Poezie* festival in Prague, like Edinburgh a UNESCO City of Literature, and inspiring them to appoint their own city poet, Sylva Fischerova. (Heady times, being able to travel!) Closer to home, I read another commissioned piece, *Edinburgh Come All Ye* - a song of oneness and inclusivity - at the Eurocities conference, again to a packed hall in the International Conference Centre.

I recall one of my predecessors as Makar, Ron Butlin, saying he'd initially been apprehensive about making these commissioned works, these occasional verses. Would he be able, as it were, to write to order? He quickly discovered he could, and in fact he found the challenge quite stimulating.

My own experience was the same. It was an opportunity to push myself. From writing mainly short poems - haiku and tanka, the odd sonnet - I stretched to longer, narrative pieces, gravitating towards traditional forms. (When I mentioned to Liz Lochhead I was writing these, she said, 'I bet they rhyme!')

Part of my brief was to write a tribute each year to the winner of the City's Edinburgh Award, and in this I took inspiration from Edwin Morgan and my teacher Sri Chinmoy, both of whom could happily turn their hand to eulogy, to singing folk's praises, when occasion demanded.

I took a great delight too in writing about the city's parks and green spaces - Arthur's Seat, St Andrew Square, Saughton Park (and even a haiku for the wee poetry tree in St Andrew Square).

Another great joy to me was working with artists. I had previously collaborated with Elizabeth Blackadder, Calum Colvin and Alison Watt (and I include here my poem *Still*, a response to Alison's altarpiece in Old St Paul's Church). As Makar I wrote poems inspired by Victoria Crowe, Doug Cocker, Rose Strang, David Williams and Joyce Gunn Cairns, all of whose images grace the book.

Covid struck halfway through my term, and I include here a blog I wrote for the Scottish Poetry Library web page on Day One of Lockdown. It links - presciently - with my last official commissioned poem as Makar, on the 'interesting times' we've lived through. The poem grew out of the Edinburgh trams project. While work was being done on the new line to Leith, it was necessary to move - temporarily! - the statue of Burns at Constitution Street. Underneath was a time capsule, placed there in 1898 (It had also been opened and re-sealed in 1961). On completion of the work, new material would be added and once again buried for future generations to discover. I was thrilled to be asked to write a poem for inclusion. I loved the idea, for what's a poem - what's any work of art - but a time capsule?

So here's a hand across the years between
for a' Jock Tamson's bairns and auld lang syne.
Know only this - we were, we lived, we loved.
Remember this. We were, we lived, we loved.

Alan Spence 2022

PASSING

Sometimes you hear a perfect sonnet line,
spoken in passing, the word on the street
fall easily but as if by design
into that good, old, pentameter beat.
So on this late September afternoon,
summer winding down, shading into fall,
the day, the year, this life, passing too soon,
I almost hear the meaning of it all
as a young mother calls out to her son
running daft in this scrap of city park.
She calls, knowing this time will soon be done,
but as if love might yet hold back the dark,
'Just play a while and then we have to go.'
Just play a while, and then we have to go.

MODERN ONE

(outdoors at Scottish National Gallery of Modern Art)

A VERY (VERY) POLITE NOTICE

PLEASE PLEASE DO
STEP ON THE GRASS.

DO NOT KEEP OUT

PLEASE DO TOUCH
THE EXHIBIT.

PLEASE PLEASE
BE HERE NOW.

THANK YOU

BORROWED LANDSCAPE

open the gate,
borrow the landscape -
it's all yours

LOCATION

YOU
ARE
HERE

INSTRUCTION

WATCH
THIS
SPACE

LANDFORM

(Charles Jencks)

landform
  shaping
      water
shaped by
      water

water
      changed
by wind
      changed
by weather

landform
      waterform

land
      water

    form

WATER / WEATHER

we

    the

        water

we

    the

    weather

LITTLE BIRD
(detail on Tracey Emin sculpture)

Can you hear it singing,
this bird that never flew?
Its song is longing.
It sings for you, for you.

It marks its little kingdom -
its name is art.
Its song is silence, freedom.
Hear it in your heart.

WORLD WITHOUT WALLS
(for Sir Timothy O'Shea)

A shilling life? Just look it up online.
The internet will give you all the facts
(though facts are not the story - yours or mine -
the story's in the words, the deeds, the acts).

Enquire within on (almost) everything -
the universe is at your fingertips.
Count angels on a pin, hear mermaids sing,
go back to the Big Bang, in youtube clips.

Just bear in mind a wise old poet spoke
of wisdom-lost-in-knowledge, knowledge lost
in too-much-information - it's no joke.
Post-truth is where we've come to - that's the cost.

But crank up your search engine anyway.
Results? Two hundred thousand at a click.
Refine your search, see what it has to say
about your subject - make it specific.

Our man's a hybrid, international -
he's German-Irish, Pole, (Silesian),
his family divided by the wall,
by politics - ugly, dystopian.

And born of that, a search for openness,
a world without walls, freedom to explore
our endless possibility, and yes,
our oneness, our humanity and more.

It started with a gift from his grandfather -
a big old taperecorder, reel-to-reel.
A machine with a memory - a wonder -
And there it was, his own, a miracle!

Fast-forward sixty years to where we are -
a nanosecond only, in real time -
but in that time he's followed his own star,
a true original, a paradigm.

He's *primus inter pares*, first among
his equals, unsurpassed, redoubtable.
His intellect is sharp, his will is strong.
The man's hard drive is incorruptible!

His universe, the university -
Open it up! Invite the whole world in!
Welcome difference, diversity
push back barriers, boundaries - begin.

There's innovation and good governance
to let imagination do its work,
the sciences, the arts joined in a dance -
light of the mind, a pure creative spark.

These massive online courses (moocs to you!)
a revolution - access open, free
available to all - can this be true?
(A million studying philosophy!)

So maybe information can still turn
to knowledge, knowledge grow into wisdom -
for that's the hope, that we love what we learn
and what we love and learn we can become.

There is no end to what we still can know.
Infinity? Beyond? Let's boldly go!

THE OLD TOWN

In a poem, in a dream, I turn and find myself
walking through the Old Town. Is it Edinburgh?
Krakow? In the poem, in the dream, it's both,
somehow, it's both at the same time.

I walk on down the Canongate to Market Square.
It's Festival time, there's jazz in the streets, poetry
in the air. I turn and find myself in a poem
in a dream. Where? Here in this bright room.

Stevenson and Conrad trade stories, tell their tales,
travellers come home at last to this place.
Milosz and MacCaig flyte, take flight, a zen calvinist,
a catholic atheist - their ideas fizz and flare.

Language is the only homeland, says Milosz.
MacCaig responds, My only country is six foot high...
Beyond the poem, the dream, the world
is turning mad, hellbent on self-destruct.

So praise them, these sister-cities of literature,
as one, Edinburgh-Krakow, Krakow-Edinburgh,
as one, holding to the dream, the poem,
to language, our homeland, our hope.

doliny, góry i rzeki -
przypadkowe
wzory wyżłobione
w kamiennym murze

Alan Spence - Edinburgh, Scotland

valleys, mountains
and rivers
the chance patterns
weathered
on this stone wall

Alan Spence - Edinburgh, Scotland

THE WELLS OF ARTHUR'S SEAT

WELLWATER

Wellwater, wellwater, now make me well.
Wellwater, wellwater, cast your bright spell.
Heal all that ails me this day, make me well,
water, pure source of all life, every cell
is full of you, made of you, so, make me well.
Wellwater, wellwater, yes, make me well.

SPRING

wellspring

        springwater

wellspring

        clearwater

clearspring

        wellwater

wellspring

        wellwater

PARLIAMENT PARKOUR

This counterterror barricade, concrete
bollards outside the Scottish Parliament -
barrier against some clear and present threat,
anticipated onslaught, bombardment -
tells us we are required to be afraid.
Forget the great architect's grand design.
Bolster defence against bomb and ramraid.
Shout Keep Out, not Welcome. Put up a sign.
But look, on this bright mild spring Saturday,
a group of children climb there, heedless, free,
learning parkour - this is a place to play,
leap lightfoot: it quickens the heart to see
them run and jump, not blocked by fearfulness,
the city, the nation, still saying Yes.

EDINBURGH COME ALL YE

From the Mediterranean to the Baltic,
from the Caspian Sea to the Atlantic,
folk have foregathered here in Edinburgh
on this bright autumn day they've come together.
In a world turned tapsalteerie, upside down
they've come from a the airts to this old town.
Let's sing a great *Come All Ye*, let it ring,
a song of peace and oneness, gathering
in strength from everyone who gives it voice,
sung clear and pure and from the heart. Rejoice
to hear it rise and swell, anthemic, free.
Our oneness is our true humanity -
this city every city, this nation
the world. Beyond all separation,
division, sing *einheit, l'unita*
unidad, aonachd jednosc, jednota...
and every other way of saying it.
Oneness. Come All Ye. Celebrate. Sing it.

THE BALLAD OF SAUGHTON PARK

Come walk with me in Saughton Park
Come walk with me a while.
Come walk with me in Saughton Park
We'll step it out in style.

Our neolithic ancestors
first settled in this place -
first farmers, fishers, foresters,
they barely left a trace

of how they lived, of who they were
that first community
beside a loch no longer there,
all ghosts, as we will be.

The name is Gaelic, seilach tun,
the place of the willow,
the willow grove. Say it - Saughton -
hear the winds sough and blow.

Centuries passed, Saughton became
a place of sanctuary -
a place of refuge, asylum,
pure healing energy.

Water of Leith, flow by, flow by.
Water of Leith, flow by.
Carry all care and grief away.
Water of Leith flow by.

The whole world came to Saughton Park
a century ago -
some visionary lit a spark
and watched it glow and grow.

The call went out, Come one, come all,
the world is welcome here.
Our nation's international -
come see what we can share.

They came, from Russia, Canada,
Japan and Senegal
from Italy and India,
from a the airts. Come all.

A festival, an exhibition,
trade fair and jamboree
in just a year three million
folk came to look and see.

On switchback railway, helter skelter
water chute and maze,
in spider's web and hall of laughter
they passed the endless days.

Before the-war-to-end-all-war
they gathered here in peace.
Before the-war-to-end-all-war
they gathered here in peace.

Water of Leith, flow by, flow by.
Water of Leith, flow by.
Carry all care and grief away.
Water of Leith flow by.

And now we're in another time,
another century.
This green space is a paradigm
of how things have to be -

a world made new, now celebrate
this re-imagining.
Walk up the path, open the gate.
to glorious flowering.

Friends of the Park, this is your place
this is your time, your day.
Skateboarders, Dreamers of Peace,
come in to play and pray.

You'll find the goddess Parvati
bestowing light and grace.
She's Mother Earth, fertility.
See her compassion-face.

The old bandstand has been restored
to what it used to be.
So get in tune now, strike that chord
and let the music play.

Come walk with me in Saughton Park
Come walk with me a while.
Come walk with me in Saughton Park
We'll step it out in style.

POETREE

wee haiku of a tree -
smallest in the garden
but holding its own

THE ARTIST
(for Joyce Gunn Cairns)

she draws you

out of

your self

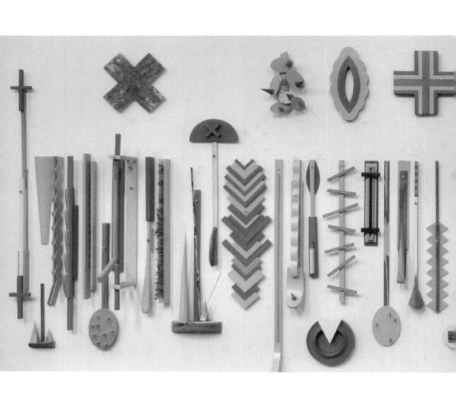

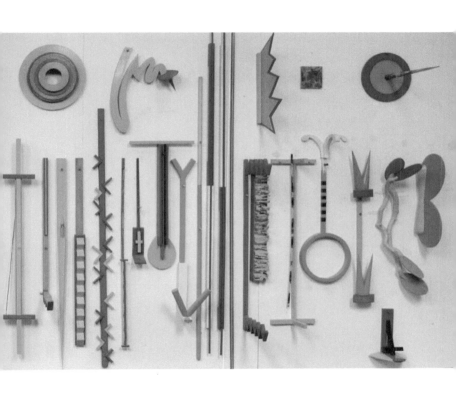

FIELD OF VISION
(Meadow by Doug Cocker).

meadow grew out of swamp was once quagmire.
art was raw colour daubed on a cave wall.
music far back was sound was noise cacophony.
now here in this bright place this bright space.
we cross a threshold enter into our selves.
take matter, material and shape it, sculpt it
keep chaos back, stand in original awe -
make this and this and this and this…
ideas in things, the *ineluctable modality*
of the visible. it's world made light the artist's field
of vision - the artist's field of vision
these objects not found but made created crafted
with care and placed just so right there
and there and there - artefact and archetype
not random not ordered finding its own form
geometric, organic, see icon symbol totem -
cross and circle, a frame within the frame.
stand back and it's landscape, opening out
come close and its music draws you further in.
a wash of sound. the colours sing, an invocation.
it is all work in progress as the universe is.

JUST A THOUGHT

D'ye reckon folk in Athens call it
The Edinburgh of the South?

STILL

(for Alison Watt)

a seamless garment

white robe hanging

in folds enfolding

time and space

folds in the fabric

a universe opening

from this still centre

state of grace

heart of the matter

flowering unfolding

white rose white rose

white rose

rose again

COFFEE SHOP HAIKU

a zen circle -
the imprint left by
my coffee cup

FLOWER OF SCOTLAND
(for Doddie Weir)

The big man in the tartan suit says Right.
This is it. He's up there, centre stage.
He's standing tall, he's standing in the light,
the absolute embodiment of courage

It's been a bit of a nightmare, he says.
Ach well. We've had a good old time of it.
But don't start singing *Thank you for the days...*
As you can see, he's here, he's no deid yet.

Far cry from Murrayfield or Twickenham
(the killing fields of Mpumalanga!)
to this new arena, public platform
(and no, the man won't look back in anger).

The pummelling, the pounding that he took,
the battering in scrum and ruck and maul -
in about him with knee and fist and boot -
gave him the strength to thole, endure it all.

You'll mind at every line-out he soared high -
he just defied belief and gravity -
and higher still he'd rise, he'd seem to fly
abune them a' he'd climb effortlessly.

And there was Bill McLaren's famous line
that stayed in the memory, made you laugh,
caught the running style to perfection -
He's on the charge like a mad giraffe

His energy's colossal, titanic,
a giant among giants, towering -
a Lion, Barbarian, heroic
a Flower of Scotland truly flowering.

He's a self-confessed fashion disaster -
the tartan suit is unforgettable.
Sartorially the man's a master
of overstatement. But he wears it well.

The tartan's colour-coded - for Scotland
blue-and-white, for Melrose yellow-and-black
Newcastle's magpie black-and-white - a grand
cacophony for maximum impact.

It's made for the new role he has to play -
ambassadorial, theatrical,
part stand-up, he can tell a joke or three.
But now he's on a mission. This is real.

Is he religious? Not especially.
But then there was the time he crashed his car -
A real bad smash, he says. Who knows what saved me -
maybe a guardian angel, lucky star?

Or maybe the Big Guy upstairs looked down,
said Haud on man, it's no your time yet. Please,
you've got a while, there's still work to be done.
So now for God's sake tackle this disease.

Just sitting waiting for the inevitable?
That's not an option, thank you very much.
Face demons down. Who knows what's possible?
Defeat? Despair? Just kick them into touch.

We sing, When will we see your like again?
Doddie, when will we see *your* like again?

SHINING

This last phase of my life -
I'm past the allotted span,
the threescore years and ten.

Now comes this blessing
this light from the East,
shining on me, shining.

Bright morning.
The rising sun.
The Rising Sun.

SEASONS (FOUR HAIKU)

spring sunshine
white swan on the water
trailing light

summer evening -
above the traffic noise,
birdsong

autumn evening -
sign in the shop window:
everything must go

written in the snow
on the car windscreen:
enough

QUEEN OF HEARTS
(for Ann Budge)

She'd aye been told football was a man's game -
a vicious bear-pit, *Nae place for lassies.*
(Of course they were the folk that said the same
about the boardroom, the pulpit…) Stasis

rules - no point in even trying to change
the way things are the way they've always been.
But this one's tough - she's up for a challenge
She's never feared to stand up and be seen.

Her friends describe her as a wee bit hard -
I'll take that as a compliment, she says.
But push it and you'll get a yellow card
(or a straight red will put you in your place!)

Glass ceiling? She shattered that long ago,
saw whole new worlds of possibility
opening up, the future in the flow
of information, new technology.

Made millions. Invested. Sold up. Moved on.
What next? Who knew? The woman had it all,
wanted for nothing. She'd been there and done
the lot. Then she responded to the call.

They used to sing, *Hearts Hearts Glorious Hearts,*
but the glory days were no more, no more.
The assset-strippers gathered, wind up merchants -
administrators waiting at the door.

A once-great club had fallen among thieves
till she stepped in, stepped up, turned things around,
created a groundswell, made folk believe.
Her eye was clear, her judgement was sound.

She could be sailing her boat in Corfu -
Koulora, Kassiopi, Kalami -
the sea, the sky a pure cerulean blue
instead she's working, here in grey Gorgie.

The boat's called *Queen of Hearts*, and by the way,
she named it in honour of her daughter -
'the only Jambo in the family.'
It cleaves the waves, rides high in the water.

Ironic that it's registered in Leith.
But Leith was where her father worked, laboured
down in the docks. It's where he cut his teeth
on girders! Leith hammered, moulded, shaped her.

And now she's crossed the gulf from East to West,
hoisted her colours, raised them high - maroon
and white, they fly. She wears the badge, the crest,
heraldic, for Heart of Midlothian.

She says Tynecastle's no place for snowflakes.
When things go wrong you just get dog's abuse.
But she can stand her ground (*her* ground, her place!)
She's here, she knows the score, she's paid her dues.

Tomorrow? Next season? Who knows, can say?
She'll be here as long as she needs to be.
Then it'll be, *Up anchor, sail away,*
leaving a legacy, a memory.

This is her story and this is her song.
This is *her* story and this is *her* song.

ALL ABOUT THE LIGHT.
(for Victoria Crowe)

Ultimately it's all about the light -
catching the light, celebrating the light,
the light of consciousness by which we see,
the light that comes at last to know itself,
the self-revealing light in everything,
within, without. It's all about the light.
Circumspice - look and the world's made new.
It's all about, it shines in the clear light.
Behold and be beholden. Look and see
the sheer particularity of things.
Snow moment. Winter fence. Numinous tree.
Considered silence. Hidden moon. Blue thaw.
Dark dog and hillside. Shape of the shadow.
Reflected contemplation. Lying snow.
Praise the everyday, the vision, the dream.
Ultimately it's all about the light.

HOW THE SNOW FELL

(sampled haiku from painting titles by Victoria Crowe)

how the snow fell -
throughout
a single day

the shortest day -
visiting cat
and two snowmen

from day to evening -
twilight
deeper shade

frozen moment -
still life with
impermanence

FROM SCOTLAND STREET
(for Alexander McCall Smith)

Open a book and you open a door,
a portal, a gateway, cross a threshold.
Rediscover hope, ye who enter here!
The writer spins a yarn of purest gold.

You step into his world and find yourself
at home, in Edinburgh, Gaborone,
listening to the tales he has to tell.
He makes the exotic familiar, known.

Just walk from Scotland Street to Zebra Drive
in the company of cheerful ladies.
Be fully open-heartedly alive
to joy and hope and love. See what he sees.

Discover the lost art of gratitude,
(See things in themselves and just as they are).
Maintain - if you can - the right attitude
to rain (and sleet and snow, sunshine and haar).

Friends, lovers, chocolate, the full cupboard
of life, a distant view of everything,
blue shoes and happiness, yes, the comfort
of Saturdays, celebrate it all, sing!

Utopian? he asks, and he'll agree,
he tends to dwell more on the positive.
than on the pathological - he'll see
the best in all, accept the negative.

His Orchestra is Really Terrible.
The clue is in the name - you have been warned.
Musically challenged but indomitable,
they play con gusto and will not be scorned!

They don't quite stay a tempo or in tune -
Keep standards low is their philosophy.
Our man's in woodwind, plays a mean bassoon,
revelling in the pure cacophony.

To him it's all precious, miraculous,
the glorious given, the everyday,
the ordinary rendered wondrous.
Like Stevenson he travels hopefully.

Sometimes you'll find him, out on the water,
between the mainland and the Hebrides -
the Sound of Mull - in his gaff-rigged cutter,
cleaving the waves, heading for open seas.

He doffs his panama hat to Auden,
to Burns, praises their deep humanity,
their empathy, insight, true compassion.
He takes delight in their good company.

The goodness of his books is manifest -
companionable as the man himself.
What shines through is an innate kindliness,
a sense that, even yet, all shall be well.

This is his gift to us, his offering.
Open the book, open the door, step in.

ON PORTOBELLO PROM

O

I do like to be

beside the sea
beside the sea

I do like

to be

It's just the way it changes

O

I do like to stroll

along the prom
along the prom

I do like

to stroll

When walking, just walk

DAY ONE

I'm writing this on day one of lockdown. The announcement that this was imminent was made by Nicola Sturgeon in a speech that was memorable for its dignity, its truth and its deep humanity, exhorting us to proceed with love and in solidarity, echoing a leader column she wrote last week in the National: 'The crisis is a re-minder of how fragile our world is. But it also shows us the power and strength of communities and of human solidarity in times when we are tested.'

I took inspiration from that, as I did from a piece by Olivia Laing in last weekend's Guardian, on the importance of art in a time of crisis, its power to remind us we are interconnected. She wrote, 'Hope is the precursor to change. Without it, no better world is possible.'

The work is to keep that flame of hope alive in ourselves.

Of course it's been difficult to deal with the conflicting messages, the ever-changing story. The pace of acceleration is alarming.

Just a couple of weeks ago I still had my writing regime - getting on with a new novel. I would work in the back room of the little bookshop my wife and I run. Last week I closed the shop, but kept my routine of writing in the back, self-isolated (aren't all artists?) behind closed doors. I felt not so much quarantined as cloistered.

Now it's a new phase and I'm working-from-home (as I always used to do). Our tenement flat is small and there's been some reorganisation required so we both have space. We're lucky in that our back window looks straight across Holyrood Park to Arthur's Seat. It's our backdrop, what the Japanese call 'borrowed landscape.' We also have the park as our back garden for those daily walks while they're still al-lowed.

The world is in meltdown and there's a strange dreamlike quality, a sense of unreali-ty, as life goes on, the sun shines, the birds are singing on a beautiful spring day. It feels like the 'phoney war' as we brace ourselves, knowing things are going to get worse. And yet, and yet…

I'm reminded of a haiku by Issa, a wonderful Japanese poet of the 18th century:

We walk
on the roof of hell,
looking at the flowers.

And it's essential to keep that focus as the pandemic rages.

A neighbour in the ground floor flat across the road has posted a message in the window, little plastic letters spelling out, TAKE CARE. BE WELL.

Our lives (like everyone else's) have become simplified. There's a concentration on what's essential and true.

We've been practising meditation now for almost 50 years, following the path of Sri Chinmoy. We always get up at 6am and meditate first thing. Now our meditations are longer, and deeper, and we spend more time singing our teacher's songs, reading his books.

Here is one of his poems, about that return to what is real in us.

Ever the same again
My lost Truth rediscovered.
Ever the same again.

Ever the same again
My forgotten Self remembered.
Ever the same again.

Ever the same again
My lost Goal regained,
Ever the same again.

INTERESTING TIMES: 2021

Remember that ancient Chinese saying -
And may you live in interesting times?
It sounds like benediction, blessing,
but no, it's contrary, not what it seems.

In fact it's wry, ironic, it's a curse,
backhanded, yes, a malediction,
a hope that things are bad and getting worse.
So here we are in 2021.

Year of the pandemic, plague, contagion,
of quarantine and sheltering in place.
Year of lockdown, shielding, isolation,
of sanitising, face-masks, track-and-trace.

Now, what to place here in this time capsule?
(*This* time, *this* place, the here and now of it).
We need the true, the real, the actual.
(History will tell the why and how of it).

A poem's a time capsule, can hold it all -
the empty city streets, the quiet skies.
You'd walk a mile and hardly meet a soul.
then see it new with suddenly fresh eyes.

Graffiti told it straight: *Hold to the light.*
And this will pass. J'existe, Keep safe. Hello.
And this, chalked up in yellow, bold and bright:
On the withered branch a new flower grows.

And somehow we survive, get through, go on,
keep fighting extinction - we're no deid yet.
The city re-awakens, the old stone
warmed by the sun. Hear the word on the street.

They'll bury this poem at the crossroads
in Leith underneath that statue of Burns,
tapping his feet in their tackety boots
to the beat, the clang of the tram as it turns.

Do you still read Burns in the far future,
still sing his songs? Do they still break the heart?
(Who else would rhyme *sever* and *forever,*
remind us that we meet only to part?)

So here's a hand across the years between
for a' Jock Tamson's bairns and auld lang syne.
Know only this - we were, we lived, we loved.
Remember this. We were, we lived, we loved.

STONES OF SCOTLAND

Stone circle overlooking Holyrood -
the palace, Parliament, Dynamic Earth -
behind it all the dramatic backdrop,
the crags, the flanks, the haunch of Arthur's Seat,
a lion, not recumbent, but *couchant*,
a great presiding presence, protective,
timeless, always changing always the same.

Up there James Hutton delved into Deep Time,
read in the strata the flow of aeons,
the planet constantly shifting, in flux,
evolving, renewing itself in fire,
beyond imagining, world without end.
Burns looked and saw *the seas gang dry, the rocks
melt wi the sun*, knew only love would last.

Walk round the circle, go *deosil*, sunwise
for good luck, or, contrary, *widdershins*
(counterclockwise, counterintuitive).
Circumambulate this whole wee country.
Step out from Shetland to the Western Isles
(grey fissile sandstone - the Broch of Mousa -
to hard band pink and grey Lewisian gneiss).

Invoke MacDiarmid, see all the loose ends
of Scotland, gathered, named, accepted, loved -
highland marble quartzite mica schist
white feldspar craigleith sandstone dark grey slate
mauchline desert sandstone black pyroxene
basalt lava medium-grained dolerite
grey crystalline granite dalradian grit

The stones are placed here by the sculptor's hand,
just so, as in an ancient zen garden.
They configure, delineate the space
make sanctuary, outlook, meeting place,
ground of being, the ground beneath your feet.
Now find your centre, your place in the world.
Know who you are and then reach out beyond.

GRATITUDE

an offering in words
but beyond words

in simple gratitude
a parting gift

intangible as light
as love

but lasting
and true

just to say
thank you

just to say
thank you

just thank you
is all

Notes

Passing

Sonnet, read at my installation as Makar. (First published in Natural Light 2 by Angela Catlin).

Modern One to Little Bird

Sequence commissioned by Scottish National Gallery of Modern Art for brochure on their outdoor sculpture space.

World without walls

Commissioned for Edinburgh Award Winner 2017, Sir Tim O'Shea

The Old town

Commissioned to celebrate link between Edinburgh and Krakow (read at Krakow Town Hall)

The Wells of Arthur's Seat

Collaboration inspired by paintings by Rose Strang.

Parliment Parkour

Inspired by Scottish Parliament Building

Edinburgh come all ye

Commissioned for Eurocities Conference, Edinburgh 2018

The Ballad of Saughton Park

Written for re-opening of Saughton Park, attended by Princess Royal

Poetree

Written in honour of Poetry Tree, St Andrew Square

The Artist

For exhibition of portraits by Joyce Gunn Cairns at Scottish Poetry Library

Field of Vision

Response to artwork *Meadow* by Doug Cocker. Commissioned by Calum Colvin for National Gallery

Still

Response to painting by Alison Watt in Old St Paul's Church. (First published by Ingleby Gallery).

Coffee shop haiku

Intended for coffee shop coasters,

Poetree

The artwork 'The Edinburgh Inch, No. 30' was printed as part of the Poems-For-All Project in an edition of 500 distributed both in Scotland and the United States.

Flower of Scotland

Commisioned for Edinburgh Award Winner 2018, Doddie Weir.

Shining

On receiving Order of the Rising Sun from Government of Japan

Queen of Hearts

Commisioned for Edinburgh Award Winner 2019, Ann Budge.

All about the Light.

Commissioned for retrospective exhibition by Victoria Crowe, City Art Centre.

From Scotland Street

Commisioned for Edinburgh Award Winner 2020, Alexander McCall Smith.

On Portobello Prom

Commisioned for Portobello Art Walk 2020, accompanying photographs by David Williams (words and images projected on wall by Promenade).

Day One

Blog commissioned by Scottish Poetry Library on first day of lockdown.

Interesting Times: 2021

Commissioned for time capsule to go under statue of Robert Burns in Leith.

Stones of Scotland

Response to sculpture at Regent Terrace Edinburgh by George Wyllie, Kenny Munro and Lesley-May Miller. Poem commissioned for Push the Boat Out festival.

Gratitude

Commissioned by Edinburgh City of Literature.

ALAN SPENCE is an award-winning poet and playwright, novelist and short story writer. Awards include McVitie Prize (Scottish Writer of the Year), Glasgow Herald People's Prize and Glenfiddich Spirit of Scotland Award. He is Professor Emeritus in Creative Writing at The University of Aberdeen, and from 2017 to 2021 was Edinburgh Makar (Poet Laureate to the City). In 2018 he was awarded the Order of the Rising Sun from the Government of Japan. With his wife Janani he runs the Sri Chinmoy Meditation Centre in Edinburgh.